*Keep on laughing!
it's better than
belly-aching.*

Pek

All the artwork and handlettering was done by a convict in the Tennessee State Prison.

"Pek" Gunn

The Author

MEMBER AMERICAN SOCIETY COMPOSERS, AUTHORS AND PUBLISHERS

State of Tennessee

Department of State

To all to whom these Presents shall come, Greeting:

I **Joe C. Carr**, *Secretary of State of the State of Tennessee, do hereby certify that the annexed is a true copy of*

House Joint Resolution No. 115 - Acts of 1970
MAKING
RICHARD M. "Pek" GUNN
Poet Laureate of Tennessee

the original of which is now on file and a matter of record in this office.

In Testimony Whereof, I have hereunto subscribed my Official Signature and by order of the Governor affixed the Great Seal of the State of Tennessee at the Department in the City of Nashville, this FOURTH *day of* FEBRUARY *A.D. 19* 70

Secretary of State

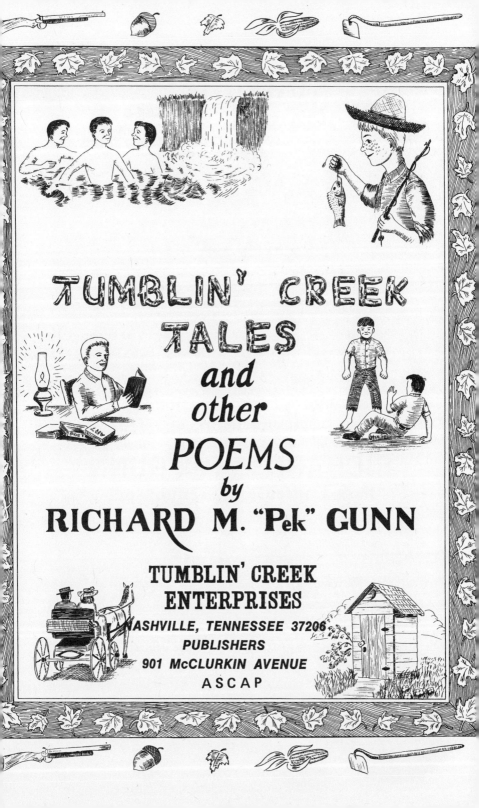

TUMBLIN' CREEK TALES
and other POEMS

by

RICHARD M. "Pek" GUNN

TUMBLIN' CREEK ENTERPRISES

NASHVILLE, TENNESSEE 37206
PUBLISHERS
901 McCLURKIN AVENUE
ASCAP

THIS COPY OF

TUMBLIN' CREEK TALES

BELONGS TO: _____

_____

PRESENTED BY: _____

_____

DATE: _____

_____

Foreword

Through this collection of verse and rhyme, Richard M. "Pek" Gunn has captured a quaintness and charm which, although often reminiscent of another age, is delightfully interwoven with both humor and pathos, making the work appealing to poetry lovers of all ages.

His devotion to humanity, the high ideals and ethical standards which he represents, together with the Christian principles which he exemplifies are reflected in these choice selections.

It is a pleasure to recommend this collection of poems by my long time friend for reading pleasure, relaxation and inspiration. I believe it will have achieved its purpose if, through its pages, the reader recalls and re-lives some of his own lighter moments and happy experiences.

FRANK G. CLEMENT

Governor of Tennessee

I'M PROUD OF MY RAISING

BY THE AUTHOR

Tumblin' Creek is a place . . . 57 miles west of Nashville, 14 miles southeast of McEwen in Humphreys county. I was reared there.

My people were share-croppers. The ground was poor and we had a hard time coaxing a living out of the soil. When I was seven, Papa gave me a hoe and took me to the cornfield and taught me to work; I'm glad now that he did. We carried our drinking water to the field in a gallon keg made of wood. Papa dug a hole in the ground and buried the keg to keep the water cool; it didn't work.

When I was 15, I hired out to a neighbor and he put me to grubbing sassafras bushes. I had no gloves; I couldn't afford them on forty cents a day and board. Anyway, there were commodities, such as coffee and sugar, that had to be bought at home, and Papa had to have his tobacco.

It was late fall. The cold wind chapped my hands and caused my fingers to burst open on the ends, in the corners at the nails. At quitting time each evening, my mattock handle was stained red with the blood that had oozed from those cracks.

As a boy, I loved baseball more than anything in the world, but there was no money for equipment. In all my life I never owned a baseball glove (a store-bought one, that is). I made one out of oil cloth and stuffed it with cotton waste. My bat was whittled from a sassafras pole; and I unraveled some old yarn socks to get thread to make a ball. I covered the ball with tops from cast-off shoes called "Grandma's Comforts." The boys at school honored me by adopting this as their official ball, and expected me to supply their demands, which I gladly did.

I loved skating, but never owned a pair of skates; the other boys laughed when I tried to skate on a pair that I had made out of wood.

I always wanted a billy goat to work to a wagon; we could have bought one for a dollar, but we didn't have the dollar; it was just as well, I guess, 'cause I didn't have the wagon, either. I longed for a pony, but a pony to me then was as possible as a private "Sputnik" today. A bicycle was something to look at, not to touch, much less ride.

I remember the first phonograph I ever saw. It had a big morning glory horn for a speaker; and the cabinet was about the size of a shoe box. It used cylinder records made of wax. It made an awful scratching sound, but we thought it was wonderful. I always liked to hear the song about "The Preacher and the Bear"; and the funny sayings of Cal Stewart. Alma Gluck could sing "I Love to Tell the Story" prettier than anyone I ever heard.

I remember the first train I ever saw and rode in. The first automobile I ever saw and rode in.

I remember the first Coca-Cola and the first iced tea that I ever drank. I remember the first pork and beans, the first macaroni, the first chili, the first Post Toasties, the first cherry pie, the first cocoanut cake, and the first ice cream cone I ever ate. I remember the first pair of overalls I ever owned, the first chew of tobacco I ever took, the first cigar I ever smoked, and the first girl I ever kissed.

In spite of all the hard times and deprivations, some of my most cherished memories center around TUMBLIN' CREEK; some of the best people I ever knew lived there; they wouldn't raise the sideboards on you; and thy'd swear to their own hurt and wouldn't lie.

Out of my experiences on TUMBLIN' CREEK I learned one great lesson, namely: "A man's life consisteth not in the abundance of the things which he possesseth," and material possessions do not bring happiness, 'cause I was happy then and all that I owned could have been bought for less than a dollar.

As I look back, I realize that TUMBLIN' CREEK was a great institution of learning; I was taught the GOLDEN RULE there.

Dedicated

To

Fran, the wife of my youth, and still my sweetheart, buddy and pal, whose tireless energy, exuberant personality and unfaltering Christian faith is an inspiration and a joy forever.

and

To

ANNA BELLE CLEMENT, whose loyalty to friends, hard work and devotion to duty are only exceeded by her gracious manner, kindly spirit and boundless patience which she exemplifies daily.

Miss Anna Belle Clement, Administrative Assistant to her brother, Gov. Frank G. Clement, was named Woman of The Year by the Tennessee Federation of Democratic Women, recently. The honor was bestowed upon her at a luncheon held in the Grand Ballroom of the Andrew Jackson Hotel, Nashville, Tenn., April 27, 1963. Richard M. "Pek" Gunn, speaker at the luncheon, presented Miss Clement with a pound cake baked by his wife, and offered the following toast to her:

The SWEETHEART of TENNESSEE

Of all the good folks that I know
  There's not a one I guess,
That has the know-how and the tact,
  Nor does a one possess
True nobleness of heart and soul
  That finds expression through
The kindness and the patience in
  All things they say and do.
Like one that's loved in Tennessee,
  As best as I can tell,
By everyone from east to west
  We call her Anna Belle.
No one can meet more folks than she
  And call each one by name,
And have each one think well of them,
  Yet treat each one the same.
She's in a class all by herself,
  And furthermore I say;
That she is sweeter than the cake
  She'll nibble on today.

Pin Hook Fishing

I want to go back one day next week
    To my boyhood home on Tumbling Creek
And sit on the mossy bank where I
    Sat and fished in the days gone by.

To be once more Mom's little man
    And carry my bait in a coffee can
Take an iron nut sinker and a twine string too
    Use an old pin hook like I used to do.

Then tie all this to a bean stick pole
    And drop my line in a clear blue hole
And I'll catch me a perch I betcha a buck
    For I'll spit on the worm just to bring good luck.

June Bug On A String

In days way back on Tumbling Creek
    The latter part of spring
'Twas sport for every boy to have
    A June Bug on a string.

The bug would fly like all the rest
    But what impressed me so
Was that the length of string controlled
    Just how far he could go.

Some might have thought that he was free
    To go his way but still
I held the string that gauged his flight
    And pulled him in at will.

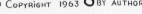

A man can get entangled too
    No matter when nor where;
And set a boundary upon
    His freedom then and there.

He may fly high and buzz about
    And have a mighty fling
But after all he's governed by
    The one that holds the string.

JERIMIAH BROWN

The biggest liar on our creek
   Was Jerimiah Brown;
His fame spread through the neighborhood
   And reached the nearby town.

A harder worker never lived,
   For he was some go-getter;
But he would lie even though the truth
   Would serve his purpose better.

He wouldn't lie to hurt a man—
   That's one good thing about it—
And what he told was just in fun,
   That's why we all allowed it.

The road-gang saw him ridin' up
 On his old horse named Nell;
They planned real quick to make him talk
 To see what lie he'd tell.

"Now, stop your horse — tell us a lie,"
 The road-gang foreman said.
"I'm sorry, but I don't have time;
 Aunt Sally Peeler's dead.

"And I'm uh-roundin' up some folks
 To dig her grave real soon,
So we can have her buryin' here
 Sometime this afternoon."

And with these words he cantered on,
　And didn't care a whit,
That work had stopped as we discussed
　Aunt Sally's death a bit.

The foreman said: "Let's store our tools;"
　And furthermore he gave
An order that we all should help
　To dig Aunt Sally's grave.

And on our way we passed her house,
　And by a patch of beans
We saw Aunt Sally, squattin' down,
　Uh-pickin' turnip greens.

The boss's temper went sky high;
  The rest tried to relieve it;
For Jerry Brown had lied again,
  And made us all believe it.

Forever after, Jerry Brown
  Would laugh and talk and rave,
And tell how we quit work to help
  Dig poor Aunt Sally's grave.

There's heaps of sorrow hereabouts;
  Some folks can't even smile;
I wish we had more Jerry Browns
  To make us laugh awhile.

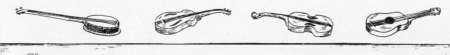

I am indebted to a former Tennessee Governor and United States Congressman, Jim Nance McCord, for the following story which I set to verse. He told me the story as I was eating breakfast with him and Mrs. McCord.

REFLECTIONS
BY
Richard M. "Pek" Gunn

In youth, temptation cried aloud
    For women, wine and song;
The things society said were the
    Epitome of wrong.

But, since "Dad", time has changed the tune
    Of all, both poor and rich;
It's Metrecal, the same old gal,
    And "Sing along with Mitch."

THREE ROOMS AND A PATH

In Nashville, every family boasts
  Of five rooms and a bath;
But in my youth I never had
  But three rooms and a path.

They built the out-house on the bank
  Of Tumblin' Creek, and then
Each time I passed, I had an urge
  To push the out-house in.

For weeks I fought this powerful urge,
  And one day I was weak—
I slipped out to the out-house, and
  I pushed it in the creek.

That night, my Dad called me aside,
  And all he had to say
Was: "Do you know who pushed the house
  Into the creek today?"

I told my Dad that it was I—
  He didn't even chide —
But then and there with leather belt
  Prepared to tan my hide.

"But, Daddy, when George Washington
  Cut down the cherry tree,
He told the truth, and so his pa
  Let little George go free."

"But, let me ask you something, son,"
  My Dad said with a frown:
"Was his pa in that cherry tree
  When Georgie cut it down?"

THE COUNTRY SCHOOL BULLY

Let me tell you 'bout the bully
   That was in our country school;
He was smart, he seemed to think
   And everybody else a fool.

He just made us do his biddin';
   Tote his dinner down the road.
We all did the things he told us
   'Cause he had us buffaloed.

He would pick on some new fellow
   When he got him out of sight,
Then he made us boys all hold him
   So he wouldn't have to fight.

He'd cuss and holler turn me loose,
   Then whisper 'neath his breath,
"Now hold me boys 'cause I have got
   This new boy scared to death."

Then little Charlie came along,
    Was new in school that day;
A humble sort of fellow —
    One with nothing much to say.

He was bashful there that morning;
    I could 'magine how he felt,
He was wearing threadbare britches
    Held up by a rawhide belt.

His blue shirt was torn and faded,
    And his hair it wasn't cut;
Had a risin' on one finger,
    And a stonebruise on his foot.

He was freckle faced and lanky;
    Bushy hair was fiery red;
He just sauntered o'er beside me,
    And I'll tell you what he said.

"Didja ever go to someplace,
    And where everybody there,
Wuz a starin' and a wonderin'
    Who ye wuz and whatche air?"

"I'm uh feelin' kinda lonesome,
    And I'd like so much to be
A friend of yourn ef you don't mind
    To be a friend to me."

"Get him out," the bully ordered,
    "Take him over by the bluff;
I wanta see what kinda metal
    This here Charlie's made out uf."

"Hello Charlie," said the leader,
    "Let's all go around the bend."
Charlie's face began to light up
    'Cause he thought he'd found a friend.

When we all got out of hearing
    Bully started to abuse;
Making fun of Charlie's clothing,
    Asked him why he had no shoes.

"Ha! Ha! look at all them patches,
    See the blue ones where they are;
Them there big 'uns on his setter
    Look like headlights on a car."

Charlie straightened up his shoulders,
    Thought he'd laugh his way on through it;
He just swallowed kinda hard like,
    Tried to smile but couldn't do it.

As I watched the little fellow
    I could tell that he was hurt;
Chin a quiverin' as he looked at
    His bare toes move in the dirt.

"Don't be laughin' at my britches,
    I'm ashamed they're all I got;
We don't have the things that you have,
    But we don't complain a lot.

"I'm gonna whoop you," said the bully,
    And he further more allowed
That he's gonna beat the stuffin'
    Outa him before the crowd.

"I'm a stranger here amongst ye,
    And I wanta do what's right;
I ain't courtin' of no trouble,
    And I shore don't wanta fight."

"Ef the things that I been sayin'
    Hurt yore feelin's in some way,
I 'pologize and beg yore pardon;
    Mama taught me thata way.

Then the bully started laughin',
    And he cut him to the core;
"You are yeller, that's yore trouble,
    I have seen yore kind before."

"This here things 'ginst my religion,"
    Charlie said, "with all my heart;
I don't want to have no trouble,
    Didn't from the very start."

"I'm a thinkin' uf my Mama
    Who would disappointed be,
Ef she knowed that I wuz fightin',
    It would hurt her don't you see?"

"Then the Bible plainly tells us
    That's no way for us to live;
Ef we git along together —
    It's a game uf take and give."

But the bully kept a ravin',
    Called him names that made us sore,
Names that he had never dared to call
    The fellers heretofore.

Charlie said, "Now I ain't likin'
    These here words I hear you say;
It's not that I'm such a coward
    That I'm actin' this-uh-way."

Then the fightin' words were spoken;
    Bully sneered, and set his jaw;
"You got feathers on yore legs, and
    Ain't no gravel in yore craw."

We were holdin' of the bully,
    Makin' out that he was bad;
Pretending if we didn't hold him,
    He would kill the other lad.

We had all agreed together,
    But the bully didn't know,
That we planned today to loose him
    'Bout the time he's rarin' so.

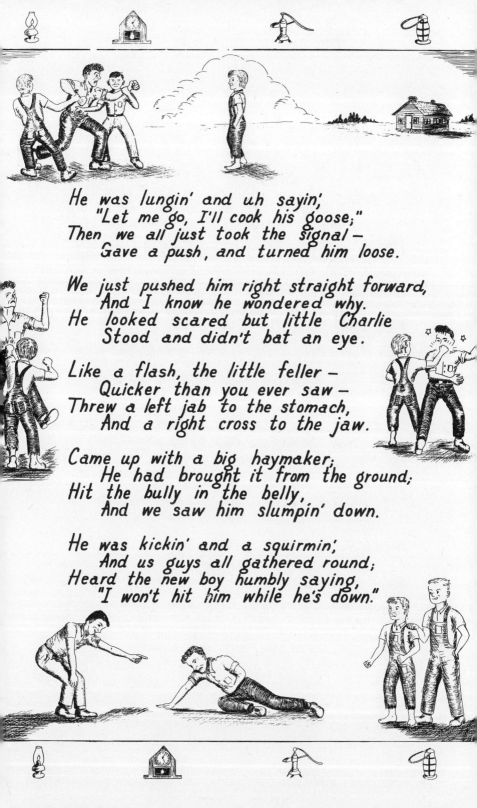

He was lungin' and uh sayin',
   "Let me go, I'll cook his goose;"
Then we all just took the signal —
   Gave a push, and turned him loose.

We just pushed him right straight forward,
   And I know he wondered why.
He looked scared but little Charlie
   Stood and didn't bat an eye.

Like a flash, the little feller —
   Quicker than you ever saw —
Threw a left jab to the stomach,
   And a right cross to the jaw.

Came up with a big haymaker;
   He had brought it from the ground;
Hit the bully in the belly,
   And we saw him slumpin' down.

He was kickin' and a squirmin',
   And us guys all gathered round;
Heard the new boy humbly saying,
   "I won't hit him while he's down."

When we all went home that evening,
    Bully toted his own books —
Girls all knowed that somethin'd happened;
    They could tell it by our looks.

We don't mind him any longer
    For there's one thing that we know —
When he jumped on little Charlie,
    Charlie killed his buffalo.

I cain't laugh when you're mistreatin'
    Other folks; I tell you why —
I just cain't see no fun in it,
    If it hurts the other guy.

You can mistreat other people,
    But you won't get very far,
Until someone will call yore bluff,
    And show you up for what you are.

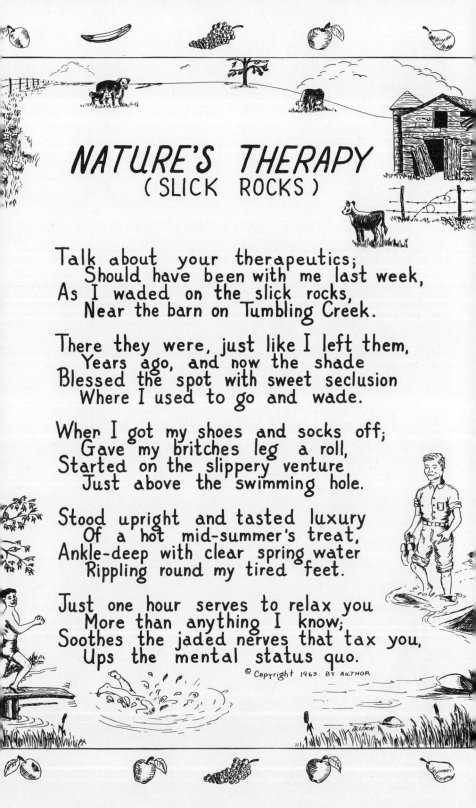

NATURE'S THERAPY
(SLICK ROCKS)

Talk about your therapeutics;
    Should have been with me last week,
As I waded on the slick rocks,
    Near the barn on Tumbling Creek.

There they were, just like I left them,
    Years ago, and now the shade
Blessed the spot with sweet seclusion
    Where I used to go and wade.

When I got my shoes and socks off;
    Gave my britches leg a roll,
Started on the slippery venture
    Just above the swimming hole.

Stood upright and tasted luxury
    Of a hot mid-summer's treat,
Ankle-deep with clear spring water
    Rippling round my tired feet.

Just one hour serves to relax you
    More than anything I know;
Soothes the jaded nerves that tax you,
    Ups the mental status quo.

ICE CREAM MAKING
ON TUMBLIN' CREEK

On the creek where my boyhood days were spent,
All ice cream making was a rare event.
You couldn't buy ice at the country store
So you had to drive your team thirty miles or more
To get the ice fixed in a sawdust pack
And have it sewed up in an old grass sack
Placed in the wagon, covered with hay;
When you got back home, you'd been gone all day.
You scrubbed the freezer with soap and sand,
And it was the kind that was turned by hand.
It seemed that the fellows hanging 'round the store
Could hear that old freezer for a mile or more;
And here they'd come, every lazy whelp,
'Til you just couldn't use all the proffered help.
They'd gather around and my face would just burn
As each insisted, "Now, let me turn!"
All down through the years I've wondered why
So many good people sit idly by
When your day is hot on a lonesome road,
And you long for some help to carry the load.
And there they'll sit, while a faithful few,
Will travel the miles in the heat with you;
Then here they'll come with an offer of aid
'Bout the time the cream is almost made.
But, you say that happened down in the sticks?
Well, I've seen it happen in politics......
                    1962 vintage, that is!

THE PEEK HOLE

Caught me lookin' through a peek-hole;
  Don't be criticizin' me;
It's the peek-hole of my memory,
  And I'll tell you what I see.

I can see my Uncle Jackson
  Way down there on Tumbling Creek;
If you'll come a little closer
  I will let you take a peek.

He's enjoyin' his tobacco;
  I can see him spit and grin,
See the amber on his mustache,
  And the brown stuff on his chin.

There he stands in his blue denims,
  Shirt and hat and brogan shoes;
These things constitute his wardrobe;
  Not the kind that you would choose.

Now the long day's work is ended;
  He retires — I hear him snore;
There is Lucy, his old shephard,
  Dozin' on the puncheon floor.

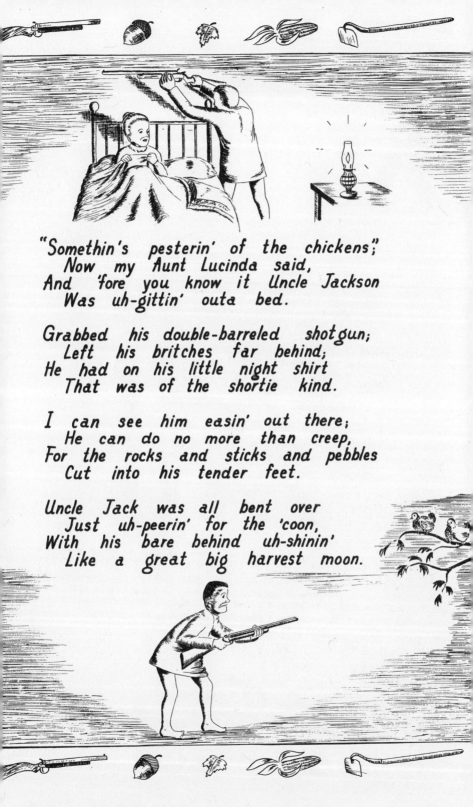

"Somethin's pesterin' of the chickens",
 Now my Aunt Lucinda said,
And 'fore you know it Uncle Jackson
 Was uh-gittin' outa bed.

Grabbed his double-barreled shotgun;
 Left his britches far behind;
He had on his little night shirt
 That was of the shortie kind.

I can see him easin' out there;
 He can do no more than creep,
For the rocks and sticks and pebbles
 Cut into his tender feet.

Uncle Jack was all bent over
 Just uh-peerin' for the 'coon,
With his bare behind uh-shinin'
 Like a great big harvest moon.

There's Aunt Cindy in her nightgown,
  Way in front of that big cur;
When old Lucy ran on past her,
  Skeered the stuffin' outa her.

"Look out, Jackson! There's the varmint!"
  But he didn't seem to mind
'Til the cold nose of old Lucy
  Tetched him on his bare behind.

Uncle Jackson jumped and hollered:
  "Lordy, get the white corn juice;
I've been bit and I'm uh-dyin',"
  Then he turned both barrels loose.

When the feathers quit uh—flyin',
  And the smoke had settled down,
There were six hens and a rooster
  Lyin' dead upon the ground.

I can see my Aunt Lucinda
  Shake her head, and hear her say:
"We got chickens for our dumplin's,
  But the varmint got away."

Now, Uncle Jack is gittin' feeble,
  But if you should want to fight—
Ask him 'bout that bunch of chickens
  That he shot one summer's night.

CONGRATULATIONS

Congratulations to you both!
    I speak as man to man;
I'm glad you won out in the race
    With Al and Rita Khan.

They say it is a lovely girl
    With smiling eyes, and then
Her cute blonde locks hang in a curl
    Above a dimpled chin.

They say she opens wide her eyes
    To look at dat and t'other;
They also tell me that she is
    The image of her mother.

Some things I just can't understand-
    It surely must be fate
While we go barren through the years,
    You populate the state.

"Congratulations" was written for and sent to my
good friends, Ed and Loraze Dozier, formerly of
Nashville, at the birth of their third baby, Pam.
This blessed event preceeded the arrival of Al
and Rita (Hayworth) Khan's baby by a few days.

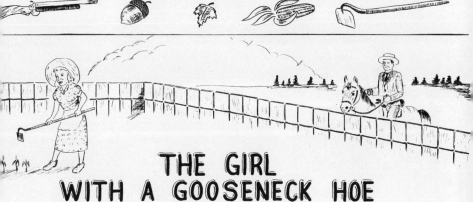

THE GIRL
WITH A GOOSENECK HOE

The garden lay beside the road,
  A palin' fence around it;
Within it stood a teen aged girl,
  And I was glad I found it.

She held a rusty gooseneck hoe,
  The weather had abused it;
The moistened armpits of her dress
  Showed plainly that she'd used it.

I wondered what I'd say to her —
  Her brown eyes were so shy;
Her limpid gaze once fixed on you
  Just made you want to cry.

Her face was tanned — her lips aglow,
  Like sumac leaves — were red;
I stopped my horse and spoke to her;
  "Hello", was all she said.

I liked her from the very start
   As she no doubt could see;
She liked me too 'cause I could tell
   The way she looked at me.

And furthermore, at my request,
   While I was standing there,
She reached and pulled her bonnet off
   So I could see her hair.

At school she slipped a gift to me—
   The teacher saw, doggone it—
A handkerchief of crepe de Chine
   With purple rings upon it

And later on down at her house
   With all her family there;
I gave my girl a jeweled comb
   That she was pleased to wear.

They oohed and aahed and talked about
   How precious jewels glow;
It didn't cost but forty cents,
   But how were they to know.

We went up to the parlor, and
   Beside an old wash stand,
I told her that I loved her and
   She let me hold her hand.

We courted on a poplar chest;
   I hate to tell you mister,
The great big tears ran down her cheeks
   Because, you see, I'd kissed her.

What would I give today if I
   Could reach back and erase
The memory of her anguish and
   The tears upon her face.

NO PARTICEPS CRIMINIS

On September 30, 1946, the following item was read in News Week magazine, to which reply was made in verse.... Tennessee "hill dialect."

"In Nashville, Tennessee, Silliman Evans, publisher of the crusading Liberal Tennessean, called in Jennings Perry, his brilliant young Associate Editor, two days after Henry Wallace's Madison Square Garden speech. Evans told Perry he wanted an editorial demanding that Wallace quit as a result of his attack on Sec. of State Burn's policy toward Russia. Perry complied, handed in the editorial, but said that if it ran, he would quit. The net result was blunt, but amicable. Evans said, 'Resignation accepted.' Perry said, 'I am a veteran of one war, and my son is a veteran of the other. I do not relish the manner in which we are talking our world into the Atomic War, and I do not choose to be a particeps criminis in that sorry business." Gunn saw the story while traveling, and the following was written from Connellsville, Pennsylvania and addressed to:

Mr. No Particeps Criminis
Cfo. De Nashville Tennessean
Nashville, Tennessee

Dear Mr. Criminis:

I'se read with personal gurgitation
  De News Week's story of yore resignation.
No Particeps Criminis! Well, dog my cat,
  Mistuh Perry, what makes you wanta talk like dat?
Still, I guess some people is just dat-a-way
  When dey got a little sumthin' dat dey wanta say,
But dese Particeps Criminis youse talkin' 'bout
  Is dangerous things, so please watch out.
Now, I don't know what de Criminis mean,
  But de Particeps is worser dan I ever seen,
'Cause nobody knows just an awful lot
  'Bout how much power de Particeps's got.
S'posin' it 'splodes! It's liable to,
  And tear de universe half in two;
Be too late den from outa dem depths
  To 'pologize for playin' with de Particeps.
Now, I'se a Southerner, thru an' thru—
  I'se proud of de things dat my big folks do—
Youse a-climbin' right up dem 'chievement steps,
  But you better quit messin' with de Particeps!

"Pek"

OH, YEAH?

You say that I'm a liar – and
    I may be – but by heck,
If I should swear you killed a man
    They'd tie a rope around your neck!

CALISTHENICAL NEGLECT

If I had worked to keep in trim
    By going often to the gym –
To exercise and swim and bowl –
    I wouldn't have this bulging roll!

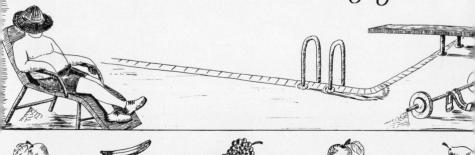

THE OPTIMIST

I passed a school on Tumblin' Creek,
    Some kids were playin' ball;
I strolled along the third base line
    Within the fielder's call.

"Say, what's the score?" I asked the chap;
    He yelled to beat the stuffin':
There's no one out, the bases full,
    And they're forty-two to nuthin'!"

"You're gettin' beat, aren't you my lad?"
    And then in no time flat,
He answered: "No sir, not as yet!
    Our side ain't been to bat!"

THE EVENED SCORE

I have lived all my life as I've found it;
  Amassed neither silver nor gold;
And I find as the years close around it,
  The things that count most, I can hold.

I have played the game fair as I've seen it,
  According to my point of view;
But realize that others who saw it
  May choose to take issue — and do.

I have seen good men pitch when their pitchin'
  Was tops, and they gave all they had;
And lost, not because of their pitching,
  But because all the fielding was bad.

Another man pitched and his pitching
  Was poor - still he got the hurrahs -
And he won, not because of his pitching,
  But because of the person he was.

I have heard the ump call 'em in pinches,
  When the game was still hanging on fate;
I've heard him scream "Out!" when by inches
  The runner was safe at the plate.

And then the scene changed with the inning;
  The grandstand came up with a shout;
The umpire yelled "Safe!" for the runner
  When everyone knew he was out.

But somehow these things will be righted,
  We reap what we sow perhaps more;
And the things that today seem benighted—
  Tomorrow will even the score.

So I've lived all my life as I've found it,
  And to me the game has been good.
Some of the players have ratted,
  But most played the best that they could.

And if you should ask me one question,
  And give me no room for to rave;
I'd have to be honest and tell you—
  I've received a lot more than I gave.

THAT HORSE AND BUGGY SCAMP

My chief competitor in love
   On Tumbling Creek was Pete;
He had a horse and buggy and
   His time was hard to beat.

He was a city dude that teased
   The girls with flattering praise,
And rubbed us guys against the grain
   With hifalutin ways.

With half closed eyes, he'd smile and blow
   The smoke rings 'bout his head.
We all smiled too but inwardly
   We wished that he was dead.

The chestnut sorrel horse he drove
   Was fast and fat and sassy;
We never would admit it but
   His rig was really classy.

It never crossed my mind that I
    Would be forced to compete,
Until one day I saw my girl
    Get goo-goo eyes from Pete.

It made me sick way down inside
    The thought stirred up my ire,
But when she goo-gooed back at him;
    The fat was in the fire.

Of course it hurt when first I learned
    Of nature's fickle whim,
And how the things a man may own,
    Can tip the scales for him.

It's hard enough to beat a guy
    Who's on a par with you;
It's harder still to have to beat
    His horse and buggy too.

I patched my heart the best I could,
    And tried hard not to show
The pain I felt and couldn't hide
    Because it hurt me so.

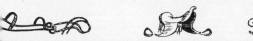

In my despair I wondered how
   That I could get to be
A lover so he couldn't take
   My girl away from me.

The Sears & Roebuck catalogue
   Revealed to me a plan,
That if I followed, I could be
   A shore nuff courtin man.

Right then I set my mind to beat
   That horse and buggy sport;
I ordered out a book on love,
   So I could learn to court.

I met the postman when it came,
   And read it through and through;
And put in practice every day
   The things it said to do.

Night after night I read that book
   Beside a coal oil lamp,
A gaining knowledge how to beat
   That horse and buggy scamp.

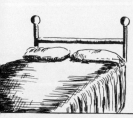

It said be kind to everything,
    And so I gave a care
To little cats and dogs and birds,
    And all things like that there.

It told me how to stroke her hair,
    And nibble on her ear,
And whisper them sweet nothings that
    The girls all love to hear.

It said to be conversant in
    The things of world renown;
Therefore I strived to learn as much
    As them there folks in town.

I read of Rome's decline and fall,
    By Gibbons; and what's more,
Of Babylon's Empire, and the states
    That touched her Chaldean shore.

I scanned the Poets; Keats and Burns,
    And Milton's words of hope;
The works of William Cullen Bryant,
    And Alexander Pope.

Then I perused the world of art;
    The works of Angelo,
Da Vinci, Rembrandt, Raphael,
    Roselli and Van Gogh.

But as I filled the knowledge pot
    A shocker came to me;
She quit the horse and buggy scamp
    And married a model "T."

This was written one Saturday morning while
Frances was preparing breakfast. A door key to
my house was enclosed and sent to four friends
in different parts of the world......

A GIFT FROM US TO YOU

When you find Nashville on your list,
    You'll need a place to stay;
Don't stop at some hotel uptown,
    Just come on out our way.

And should you drive up to our house,
    Approach the door, and then
You knock and find us not at home;
    This key will let you in.

Now, don't be bashful at that time,
    Just use your thinking dome:
Unlock the door, bring in your bags,
    And make yourselves at home.

For we'll be back ere very long;
    Please stay, for goodness' sake,
And soon you'll hear the sizzlin' sound
    Of steaks upon the grate.

A charcoaled, rare — rye bread and tea —
    With trimmin's, my they're good!
And soon your jaws will work just like
    A jersey chews her cud.

It gives us pleasure now as we
    This key to you impart:
'Tis emblematic of the one
    You folks hold to our heart.

LYE HOMINY

There are heaps of tasty victuals
    That are made in different ways;
You should eat some old lye hom'ny
    Mama made from Indian Maize.

Now, she seldom ever made it,
    For the job was very tough;
If you listen I will tell you
    Just how Mama made the stuff.

First, she rose up bright and early,
    At the breaking of the morn;
Then we went up to the crib and
    Shucked about two pecks of corn.

We would pick it and we'd cull it,
    Take the grains from off the cob;
Give a portion to old Dobbin
    And a little to old Bob.

Then we'd take what we selected,
     Put it in a flour sack —
Tie it — swing it 'crost my shoulder,
     And I'd come on struttin' back.

Now, I'd start to fill the kettle
     With the water I would bring;
Then I fetched a sack of ashes,
     And she tied it with a string.

When the water started boilin'
     And we knew that it was hot,
She would drop the corn and ashes
     To the bottom of the pot.

I could see the bubbles jumpin'
     And cavortin' all aroun',
Then the lye came from the ashes
     And it turned the water brown.

Then the grains would turn right yellow
　　As we boiled it most of morn,
And the lye would swell the kernels,
　　Eat the husk from off the corn.

If we boiled it for a while and
　　Found the husk just wouldn't give:
Mama took it out and rubbed it
　　In the bottom of a seive.

"Quit yore eatin' them raw kernels!"
　　Mama said, "For goodness' sake!"
"Too late now," for I'd already
　　Eat so much my tummy ached.

"Come here, Dicky," said my Mama,
    Fetch the tub from off the stump."
Mama always let me help her
    Take it to the village pump.

There I'd work the big iron handle,
    Watch the water start to spurt;
Then she washed the grains of hom'ny
    Whiter than a Sunday shirt.

You can't buy no store bought hom'ny-
    Makes no difference what you paid-
That will ever have the flavor
    Like the kind that Mama made.

In 1955, Governor Frank G. Clement told the author that he was going to appoint him to a position on the Governor's staff. Christine Reynolds was Welfare Commissioner at the time. The appointment was delayed — Gunn waited patiently. One day, Governor Clement received the following letter from Gunn:

BY WAY OF REMEMBRANCE

My Dear Governor:

Perhaps I shouldn't tell you this,
But really you should know,
That beans and 'taters at my house
Are gettin' pretty low.

And if my present state persists—
It is my firm belief—
That friend Christine will have to give
Me some sort of relief.

"Pek"

NOTE: Gunn got the appointment next day!

PICKLEMENT

When I came to the city, boys,
　　I sure was in a pickle;
For deep down in my pockets I
　　Couldn't even find a nickle.

But I determined to succeed,
　　And started out to run
At doing things so I could make
　　My place up in the sun.

Now take a look at me today;
　　I reckon now as how
That I have been successful, 'cause
　　I've got a nickle now.

YELLOW DOG DARE

With Grady, and Dick, and Mooney, and Jim,
  In Tumbling Creek for a country swim;
In days way back when a kid down there
Was a yellow dog if he took a dare.

Dick, climbed a tree -- stood on a limb,
  And Mooney, hurled a dare at him;
He 'lowed he wouldn't take a dare,
  So he dived right in from away up there.

And as he hit, kersplash he went,
  But he struck his head on a piece of flint;
His body went limp - we thought he was dead,
  For the blood gushed out and the creek turned red.

We pulled him out and headed for home;
  Our hearts were glad when we heard him moan,
And drawl from beneath a glassy stare;
  I told ye I wouldn't take a dare.

Now I've been hurt a time or two
  By jumpin' when one dared me to;
Didja know some folks will dare ye to do
  Exactly the thing they want ye to?

And some will yellow dog dare ye to
  Do the thing they're 'fraid to do
Now I ain't got much sense I know,
  But I've quit jumpin' for to make a show;
If it's dangerous to jump from where ye air,
  I figure it's best just to take the dare.

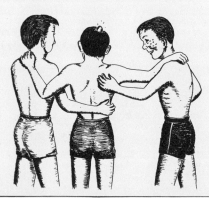

TRADIN' COMPLIMENTS

One time, on Tumblin' Creek, we used
   Some real good common sense,
When all joined in a popular fad
   Called "tradin' compliments."

We had no time for gossipers
   Who formerly held sway,
And led the conversations down
   A detrimental way......

Who kept the minds of folks abused,
   And pushed the practice further,
By tellin' things that made each one
   Suspicious of the other.

But when the tradin' fad appeared,
   We all rejoiced in givin'
Expression to our dormant thoughts
   That made a life worth livin'.

Then all of us were happy, for
   Throughout the neighborhood
The folks were tradin' compliments,
   And everyone felt good.

But then some folks began to cheat—
   To make the matter worse—
They told some things that threw the game
   Right smack dab in reverse.

Now, Affie Tummins puffed us up
   With things she said she'd heard;
When asked who told her she would say:
   "Ah, just a little bird."

And Billie Ringtom cheated, too;
    I'd trade her first, then she
Would hum and haw and finally say:
    "You'll have to credit me."

Just goes to show there are some folks
    A little short on knowin'
The proper thing to do when they
    Have got a good thing goin'.

The gossipers seemed happy, but
    Regardless of pretense —
The happiest folks down there were they
    Who traded compliments.

GRISELDA

Aunt Mandy was a patient soul,
 Or so we thought, 'til she
Spanked my little sister — then
 She grabbed a-hold of me.

I screamed and hollered, and she said:
 "Now, keep your big mouth shut!"
I sassed her and she took a strap,
 And tanned my little butt.......
 Oh, Griselda!

RETRIBUTION

I went down to play with Andy
I was dressed up like a dandy
Had a little sack of candy
　　Thinking of an undone chore
　　I was guilty once before.

Then that night it was uncanny
How my little gray haired Granny
Laid it on my little fanny
　　Put me in the bed to snore—
　　Bread and water—nothing more.

RIDE, MAN, RIDE!

I'd like to see the one who said,
  "Breathes there a man with soul so dead,"
Sit up and watch these guys refuse
  To answer questions as they choose.

I'll bet he'd take his pen and write
  A sonnet such as would indict
All those who will not take a stand
  And give allegiance to this land.

I care not if he's this or that,
  Republican or Democrat;
True citizens are honor bound
  To stand upon a common ground.

Where would we be had Paul Revere
  Refused to ride because of fear,
And failed in what he knew was right
  By snoozing in his bed that night?

Take courage, man! Use might and main.
  We stand at midnight once again;
The lantern in the tower is tied,
  So saddle up your horse and ride!

THE OLD ASH HOPPER

Ever see an old ash hopper?
   We had one down on the farm;
It was settin' 'gainst the garden
   By the footpath to the barn.

Things that came from that old hopper
   Now are only found in stores;
But I remember from that hopper
   Came the things that eased our chores.

There was good lye soap a-plenty;
   We would scrub the floors anew,
Wash our hair and do the laundry,
   Use it for our bathing, too.

When at times the hogs got wormy—
  Papa said they had the squirms—
Fed 'em lye right from the hopper,
  And that made 'em pass the worms.

We used lye at our hog killin's,
  Put some in the scaldin' trough,
When we dipped the hogs down in it,
  It would make the hair come off.

Then it served another purpose,
  Lye was used for certain ills;
I'm forbidden to disclose it—
  It's a secret of the hills.

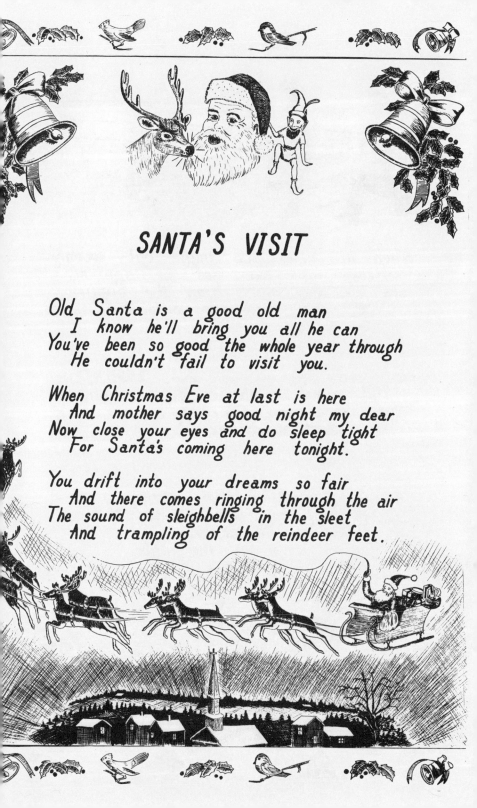

SANTA'S VISIT

Old Santa is a good old man
　　I know he'll bring you all he can
You've been so good the whole year through
　　He couldn't fail to visit you.

When Christmas Eve at last is here
　　And mother says good night my dear
Now close your eyes and do sleep tight
　　For Santa's coming here tonight.

You drift into your dreams so fair
　　And there comes ringing through the air
The sound of sleighbells in the sleet
　　And trampling of the reindeer feet.

Oh, look! there's one with nose of red,
  He leads the pack that pulls the sled
Across the fields of snow and ice;
  Old Santa thinks he's mighty nice.

There's Dancer, Prancer, strong and straight;
  Comet and Vixen at the gate;
While Blixen reaches for a limb,
  Old Donner looks across at him.

There's something new beneath the moon
  For reindeer now have learned to spoon;
There's Cupid, shy in her new fur,
  And Dasher making eyes at her.

The sleigh is piled with lovely toys
 For all the good little girls and boys;
We hear Old Santa's merry call,
 And Rudolph starts to climb the wall.

Upon the roof Old Santa stops,
 He grabs his bag and down he drops,
And pays a visit to the beds
 To peek at all the sleepy heads.

I hear him say: "They never knew
 The rain and sleet that I passed through;
The rivers crossed; the snow and ice,
 To bring them presents — oh, so nice!"

"But they've been good, I've heard of them;
  I'll fill their stockings to the brim,
'Cause I've been working through the year
  To bring them all this Christmas cheer."

He jumps into his waiting sleigh,
  And as he does I hear him say:
"Be good my dears with all your might;
  I'll see you on next Christmas night."

And with his joyous Ho! Ho! Ho's!
  He cracks his whip and away he goes;
With jingling bells he's homeward bent
  But no one knows which way he went.

At last you wake on Christmas morn,
  You hear the tooting of a horn
But where's the snow I hear you quiz
  Why that's as real as Santa is.

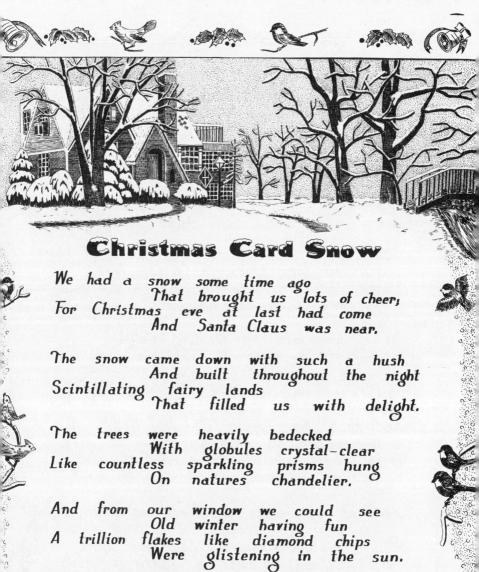

Christmas Card Snow

We had a snow some time ago
　　　　That brought us lots of cheer;
For Christmas eve at last had come
　　　　And Santa Claus was near.

The snow came down with such a hush
　　　　And built throughout the night
Scintillating fairy lands
　　　　That filled us with delight.

The trees were heavily bedecked
　　　　With globules crystal-clear
Like countless sparkling prisms hung
　　　　On natures chandelier.

And from our window we could see
　　　　Old winter having fun
A trillion flakes like diamond chips
　　　　Were glistening in the sun.

The redbirds and the chickadees
　　　　A-dartin' here and there
Gave color to the whiteness
　　　　Of the snowflakes in the air.

Our place was like a wonderland
　　　　For all about the yard
Were lovely scenes like artists paint
　　　　Upon a Christmas card.

　　　　© Richard M. "Pek" Gunn

CHRISTMAS WISHES

Within your home this glad Yuletide
  Our wish for you   shall be,
That happiness and joy abound
  Around your Christmas tree.

And as you celebrate this year,
  May every heart be thrilled;
As those you love find that each hope
  And wish has been fulfilled.

Then as the clock hands move along,
  And day fades into night;
May blessings that have come to you
  Make Christmas very bright.

We wish for you in future life,
  And those that you hold dear,
The same old Merry Christmas, and
  A prosperous, glad New Year.

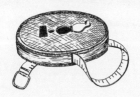

THE YARDSTICK

You won't go very far,
 If the person you are,
  Is not trusted
    And true and tried;
And I'll wager a guess
 That the door to success
  Will be closed,
    And your entrance denied.

You can go mighty far,
 If the person you are,
  Is trusted
    And tried and true;
And the door to success
 Will be open, I guess,
  And the keeper will
    Pass you right through.

— INTEGRITY —

TELL ME NOT

Tell me not that I have prayed in vain;
That sins once repented of, confessed,
Will rise to haunt me o'er again......
                                    Tell me not.

Tell me not that love so richly given
Will ever mock my soul's most earnest cry,
Nor block my way to heaven......
                                    Tell me not.

WHY?

(Tell me if you know)

Tell me why a man will sever
   Sacred ties that serve to bind
Christian men to good behavior,
   And a peaceful state of mind.

Spurn the very ones that love him;
   Crush the hearts of those who care;
Scorn the faithful friends that lift him
   Daily to the throne in prayer.

Forage for forbidden pleasures,
   Such as always take their toll;
Daily add like prison shackles
   Weights of hindrance to the soul.

Rationalize his strange behavior,
   Blame another for his plight;
Play the cynic as he strays from
   Paths of rectitude and right.

SUPPLICATION

"Blessed are the pure in heart for they shall see God."
Jesus

Give me a heart so pure that I
  Will see my God in everything....
Not only in the prosperous days,
  But in reverses life may bring.

A heart submissive to his will
  When sunny days give way to rain;
Such blessings count of equal worth
  As those based on material gain.

A heart that clings, though paths are dim,
  And cherished hopes have turned to dust;
A heart so fixed, though slain by him,
  Will still give praise and dare to trust.

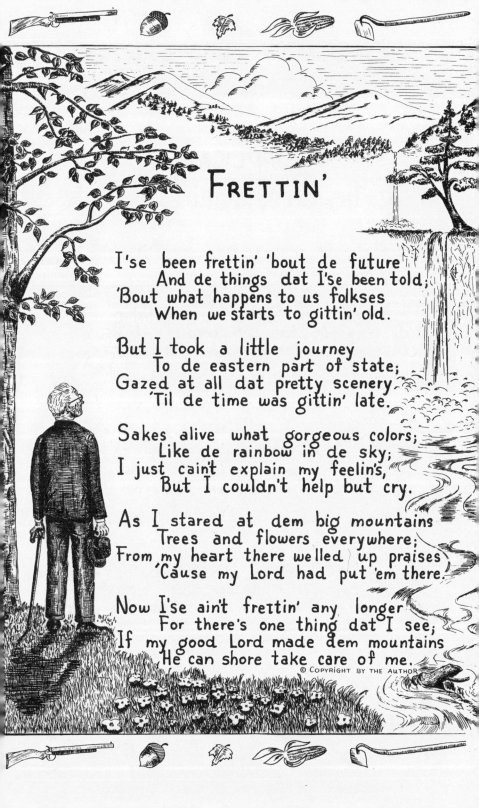

FRETTIN'

I'se been frettin' 'bout de future
    And de things dat I'se been told;
'Bout what happens to us folkses
    When we starts to gittin' old.

But I took a little journey
    To de eastern part of state;
Gazed at all dat pretty scenery
    'Til de time was gittin' late.

Sakes alive what gorgeous colors;
    Like de rainbow in de sky;
I just cain't explain my feelin's,
    But I couldn't help but cry.

As I stared at dem big mountains
    Trees and flowers everywhere;
From my heart there welled up praises
    'Cause my Lord had put 'em there.

Now I'se ain't frettin' any longer
    For there's one thing dat I see;
If my good Lord made dem mountains
    He can shore take care of me.

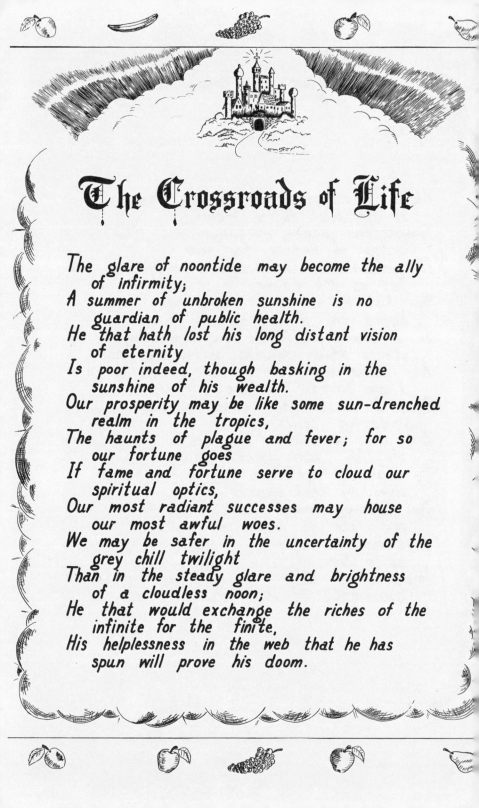

The Crossroads of Life

The glare of noontide may become the ally
   of infirmity;
A summer of unbroken sunshine is no
   guardian of public health.
He that hath lost his long distant vision
   of eternity
Is poor indeed, though basking in the
   sunshine of his wealth.
Our prosperity may be like some sun-drenched
   realm in the tropics,
The haunts of plague and fever; for so
   our fortune goes
If fame and fortune serve to cloud our
   spiritual optics,
Our most radiant successes may house
   our most awful woes.
We may be safer in the uncertainty of the
   grey chill twilight
Than in the steady glare and brightness
   of a cloudless noon;
He that would exchange the riches of the
   infinite for the finite,
His helplessness in the web that he has
   spun will prove his doom.

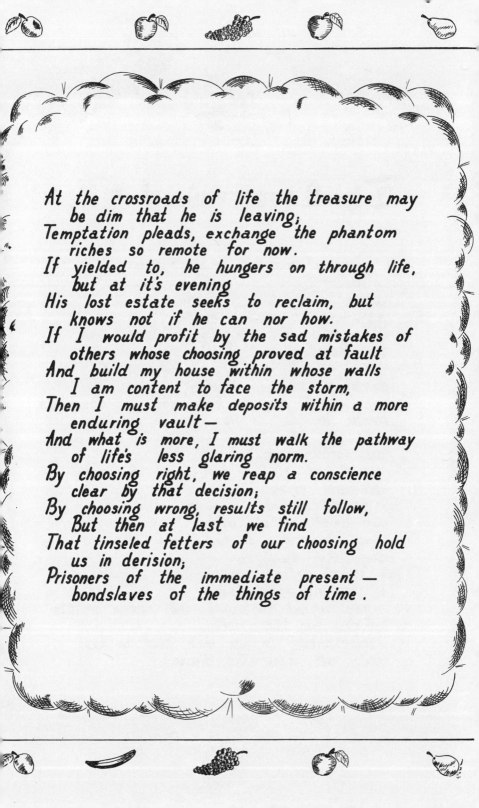

At the crossroads of life the treasure may
    be dim that he is leaving;
Temptation pleads, exchange the phantom
    riches so remote for now.
If yielded to, he hungers on through life,
    but at it's evening
His lost estate seeks to reclaim, but
    knows not if he can nor how.
If I would profit by the sad mistakes of
    others whose choosing proved at fault
And build my house within whose walls
    I am content to face the storm,
Then I must make deposits within a more
    enduring vault —
And what is more, I must walk the pathway
    of life's less glaring norm.
By choosing right, we reap a conscience
    clear by that decision;
By choosing wrong, results still follow,
    But then at last we find
That tinseled fetters of our choosing hold
    us in derision;
Prisoners of the immediate present —
    bondslaves of the things of time.

THE OLD PRAYER MEETING

Not just for now, but through the years,
    Our friends we have been greeting
Each week when they all gather in
    Down at the old Prayer Meeting.

Dave Thompson will be there, I know,
    And so will Brother Bennett;
Nor would the service be complete
    Unless John T. was in it.

Just look for Brother James A. Pate —
    His faithful family four —
His wife has played the organ there
    For thirty years or more.

The testimonies of the saints
    Bring gladness to my heart;
They tell of battles they have won
    In which I've had a part.

The frosts of many winters have
  Turned locks from brown to grey,
But light upon their faces show
  They're happy in this way.

When Sister Irvin testifies,
  She says: "I'm still a-standing.
It matters not what comes or goes,
  I mean to make the landing."

We love to go each Wednesday night,
  Regardless of the weather;
It makes you feel so peaceful like
  When good folks get together.

When years have served to dim my sight,
  And time is swiftly fleeting;
Oh, let my steps each week still turn
  Down to the old Prayer Meeting.

Greetings

In 1959, the author promoted and ran a special train (his 6th, sponsored by Gov. Frank G. Clement) to the Billy Graham Crusade in Indianapolis. At the meeting, Cliff Barrows introduced Gunn to 17,000 people, and asked him to say something. "Pek" responded with the following, which he had written and memorized since coming to the platform. The house came down on the first verse:

From rolling plain to shady dell —
   Where'er our people be —
I bring you "Hoosiers" greetings from
   The state of Tennessee.

Our trains have run to New Orleans,
   Louisville and the Empire State,
Charlotte, Indianapolis, and
   We've rolled to the Golden Gate.

NOTE Turning to Billy Graham, he concluded his remarks:

Our hearts are with you Billy Graham,
   Where'er your crusades be;
Just look for us — for we'll be there —
   With a train from Tennessee.

At Graham Crusade In Los Angeles

30,000 Cheer Tennesseans

LOS ANGELES—A crowd of 30,000 persons cheered mightily Sunday afternoon for a group of 212 Tennesseans who came all the way from Nashville to attend the BILLY GRAHAM Crusade Meeting in the Memorial Coliseum here.

Leaders of the Tennessee delegation were brought to the platform and introduced by BILLY GRAHAM's song leader, CLIFF BARROWS.

This is the ninth year a special trainload of Tennesseans has attended one of the Crusades.

BILLY GRAHAM stepped forward to comment that the Tennesseans have been coming so long he feels he should consult with them when he plans a Crusade.

Presented to the huge audience were RICHARD M. "PEK" GUNN, General Chairman, originator and promoter of the Tennessee trains, and his Co-Chairmen, THE REV. JAMES M. GREGG and HOWARD HOOPER. Rev. Gregg and Hooper explained that the Tennesseans had been so impressed when BILLY GRAHAM conducted his Crusade in Nashville in 1954 that their prayers had been with him for the success of all later Crusades.

But it was GUNN who brought the house down three times in a two-minute speech when he told the crowd the train had the sponsorship of GOVERNOR FRANK G. CLEMENT and then gave them the following poem:

From rolling plain to shady dell —
   Where'er our people be —
Governor Frank G. Clement sends greetings from
   The state of Tennessee.

Our trains have run to New Orleans,
   Louisville and the Empire State;
Charlotte, Indianapolis, and
   We've rolled to the Golden Gate.

To the Windy City, Chicago, and
   Miami in the Everglades;
To Los Angeles where the Pacific bathes
   The feet of the Palisades.

Our hearts are with you, Billy Graham,
   Where'er your crusades be;
Just look for us — for we'll be there —
   With a train from Tennessee.

THE PARKING TICKET

Gunn, the author, was given a ticket for an overtime parking violation. He mistakenly thought the fine was $1.00, instead of $2.00. He sent his check for $1.00 to the Traffic Violations Bureau with the following rhyme, a copy of which was also sent to the Mayor of Nashville:

"Past four – No parking", said the sign,
    But they won't catch me just this time;
And so I ran inside to see
    The one who was to ride with me.

I didn't go so very far,
    But hurried right back to my car;
A cop with pencil I could see,
    With yellow pad upon his knee.

"Hold on", I said, "don't make that mark!
    I had to have some place to park."
Said he: "You see those signs galore?
    You cannot park here after four."

With steady hand he wrote it down,
    In spite of my unhappy frown.
I asked him please to let me be;
    He still the ticket gave to me.

Then "Sarge" on motorcycle blue
   Came breezing down the avenue,
And said: "You move that pile of tin,
   Or let the wrecker pull it in!"

There I stood, with drooping head;
   I knew he meant just what he said.
I didn't want it done that way,
   So I just moved my Chevrolet.

I have no wish here to malign
   The officers in duty's line;
For I was wrong and they were right,
   And who was I to start a fight?

They tread the streets in broiling sun,
   Always polite to everyone;
Their work is harder, don't you see,
   Because of fellows such as me.

Don't take it that these cops are bad —
   No finer has a city had.
I've stretched the truth in just one line,
   But — this here verse just had to rhyme.

Three days later, Gunn received a card from the Traffic Violations Bureau with the following:

Dear Mr. Gunn:
    Parking ticket #46208, issued to you July 30, carries a penalty of $2.00. We are holding your check for $1.00 until you send another $1.00 to complete this case. At the bottom of the card it read:

This little card I hate to mail,
    But our traffic tickets are still on sale;
So send to us another buck,
    And next time I hope you have more luck.

To this, Gunn replied, sending another letter to the Mayor with all the correspondence:

Dear Mr. Halmontaller:

Your splendid verse arrived today,
    And here is all I have to say:
Thanks for the wish for my good luck,
    But why should I send you a buck?

If evidence you will supply,
    And give me some good reason why
That I should one more dollar pay,
    My check will then be on it's way.

To which Rhymester Halmontaller replied:

Dear Mr. Gunn:

Traffic ticket #46208,
  Issued to you at an earlier date,
It says: "No parking – four to six,
  And these signs I didn't help to fix.

But I agree with them, as we all know,
  It keeps the traffic on the go.
So send to us another buck,
  So we can clear this matter up.

From Gunn came the finale, and the "one
more buck" with the following:

Dear Mr. Halmontaller:

The evidence requested, sir,
  Your answer did disclose;
My check for one more dollar now
  I do – herewith enclose.

Regardless of how much the fee —
    Forbid that I should bark —
Had I been born across the sea,
    I'd have no car to park.

I think of millions that would give
    A ransom, oh, so free,
Could they exchange their way of life
    With one the likes of me.

Sometimes the freedoms we enjoy
    We do for granted take;
And sometimes fail to realize
    The laws we help to make.

And though I've had to pay the fine,
    I sure had lots of fun;
I thank you, sir; I'm truly yours .....
    Signed — Richard M. "Pek" Gunn.

The next day, on the front page of the
Nashville Banner, a two column spread carried
all the above with the catchy caption:
"Next Time You Park, Wait 'Til After Dark!"

I'VE TRIED IT IN A THOUSAND DIFFERENT WAYS

Richard M. (Pek) Gunn

Oh, you told me to for-get you, And to find some-bo-dy else,

That some one else would bright-en up my days. But I can-not love an-

oth-er And I nev-er can for-get Tho' I've tried it in a thous-and diff'rent ways.

O-MISS AGNES

C   Words music by Richard M. (Pek) Gunn

(Oh, Lawd-y) Oh! Miss Ag-nes, just look what a fix you're in; (Bm Bm Bm)
Oh! Pro-Fu-mo just look what a fix you're in; (Bm Bm Bm)

Oh! Miss Ag-nes, you just don't know where to be-gin; You went to the
Oh! Pro-fu-mo you just don't know where to be-gin; you met Chris-tine

riv-er, but you could-n't get a-cross, You paid five dol-lars for an old gray
at the swim----ming----pool-------- and then you start-ed out to play it

hoss, Yuh got 'im in the riv-er, and he would-n't swim, And you
cool, you took her around every where you went and then

beat him to death with a Sy-ca-more limb; (Bm, Bm, Bm) Oh! Mis Ag-nes!
you lied to the Par---lia----- ---ment (Bm, Bm, Bm) Oh! Pro-fu-mo!

Just look what a fix you're in! (Bm, Bm, Bm, Bm)
just look what a fix you're in! (Bm, Bm, Bm, Bm)

RED ROSE IN YOUR HAIR

R.M.G.

© Richard M. (Pek) Gunn

Take this bou-quet of red ros-es, Tie one in your love-ly hair,

To re-mind you of the days that used to be. _____ When your

heart and mind dis-clos-es That there's no one left to care,

Let your mem-'ry pay a vis-it back to me. _____

CHORUS

Tho' the snows of man-y win-ters may have streaked your hair with gray, But the

years could not im-pair your ra-diant smile; Take a

red rose from this bo-quet, Place one in your love-ly hair And in

mem-'ry come and vis-it for a-while.

THERE ARE TEARS ON MY PILLOW TONIGHT
WORDS AND MUSIC BY RICHARD M. "Pek" GUNN

Janie was fair, with soft raven hair;
She seemed to be happy and free.
Buddy, her lad, was a soldier boy clad
In khaki, far over the sea.
She heard from her boy, it brought her much joy;
His letters, one came every day.
Jane tried to smile, but after a while,
On her pillow, we heard Janie say:

1. There are tears on my pil-low to-night; My world does not seem so bright. I'm
2. There are tears on my pil-low to-night; Your kiss would make things just right. At

miss-ing you so, Just want you to know how I've prayed for you, dear, each night. Your
times my heart sings But lone-li-ness brings all the tear drops that fall to-night. I've

pic-ture is fad-ed and worn, Where I've kissed it each night and morn. I
tried to be brave it is true, But my heart is so hung-ry for you. I

love it that's true, But still it's not you, There are tears on my pil-low to-night.
want you so dear, If you were just here, To dry tears on my pil-low to-night.

············· INTERNATIONAL COPYRIGHT 1952 BY AUTHOR

TACKY KHAKI

Richard M. (Pek) Gunn

1. I may look tack-y in my khak-i, But I'm a sol-dier an-y-how;
2. I may look tack-y in my khak-i, But I'm a sol-dier an-y-way.

With my shoes too large and my coat too small and my bree-ches they're a wow.—
If you want to see me do the dou-ble quick, Just— wait till I get my pay.—

But when I get blitzed up and my pass — to town and I be-gin a set-tin' these
— With my thirty good bucks stuck down in my jeans, a gal in my— arms that's still

G. I.'s down, You ought to see them pret-ty gals peep-in' a-round, Look-in' at these
in her teens, I'm serv-in' my country to the best of my means, Wear-in' these

sol-dier clothes
sol-dier clothes

DEAR LITTLE GIRL IT'S YOU

Words and Music Richard M. (Pek) Gunn

Dear lit-tle girl, I want the world to know that I love you;

You are so neat, so per-fect-ly sweet, You are my dreams come true;

I i-dol-ize your smil-ing eyes, Your ra-diant hair, and too,

1. You are a part of my life and my heart, Dear lit-tle girl, it's

D.C. **2.** you. life and my heart, Dear lit-tle girl, it's you! Fine.

PLEADING PRAYERS

Vs. 1-4 "The Call"
V. 5 "The Answer"

Words & Music by Richard M. Gunn

1. There was a time when you, too, loved the Sav-iour, His will was al-ways your supreme de-
2. The way you go is filled with disappointment, Your deeds today, to-mor-row you will
3. If you could give me wealth as mor-tals count it, And pleasures bo't with gold or tinseled
4. I've prayed so hard and long for your re-turn-ing, And yet my pray'r seems lost, the way is
5. Man can weigh the stars of Heav-en in a bal-ance; He can count the grains of wheat in shock or

light. I would give this world to hear you sing His prais-es With a heart filled with His
meet. The influence of your life that once you cherished Now you scat-ter by the
fame, I would glad-ly give them all to hear you whis-per As once you did of
dim; But I'll trust Him tho' it seems I'm not re-ceiv-ing, He is faith-ful and will
stack; But He fails in His at-tempt to fix a val-ue On those earn-est, plead-ing

love this ver-y night.
way-side at your feet.
Je-sus, bless His name.
bring you back to Him.
pray'rs that bro't me back.

Come on back, oh come back to the

Sav-iour; He will heal your bro-ken heart and cleanse your sin. He will

dry the fall-ing tears, He'll for-give the wast-ed years, And re-

store the peace that once you had with-in.

Calling For Thee

Music of verse from old American melody

RICHARD M. (PEK) GUNN

1. If you have grown tired of your wand'ring and liv-ing in sin,
2. If you have grown care-less and lost the great joy you once had,

If you de-sire a new change in your life to be-gin;
If you have stum-bled and car-ry a heart that is sad;

Just come to the Sav-iour, re-pent of your sins and be clean,
Re-mem-ber the Shep-herd is climb-ing o'er moun-tain way steep,

For Je-sus is read-y and wait-ing your soul to re-deem.
To find and bring back to the fold His poor wan-der-ing sheep.

CHORUS

Call-ing for thee, call-ing for thee, Let Him come in, be free from your sin; O-pen the door re-ject Him no more, Just o-pen your heart and let Je-sus the Sav-ior come in.

My Sunday School

Richard M. Gunn

Richard M. Gunn
John T. Benson

1. I love to go to my Sun-day School, Listen to teach-er and pray;
2. Oth-ers should come to my Sun-day School, Who do not go a - ny-where;
3. I love to give to my Sun-day School, They have ex-pens-es to bear;

I love to learn a - bout Je - sus, It helps me a - long life's way.
They need to hear a - bout Je - sus, And of those mansions fair.
I bring my tithes to the store-house, I give to see oth - ers share.

I love to get to class ear - ly, a - bide by the gold - en rule;
They need some one to speak to them, to teach them the gold - en rule;
I'll bring my gifts to the Mas - ter and prac-tice the gold - en rule;

So I'll get up and get start-ed on time to my Sun-day School.
I'll go in - vite and bring some-bod-y else to my Sun-day School.
I'll work, I'll save and bring mon - ey to give to my Sun-day School.

ROY ROGERS—DALE EVANS—BILLY GRAHAM
FETED BY TENNESSEANS

Los Angeles, August 21, 1963—ROY ROGERS and his equally famous wife, DALE EVANS, joined BILLY GRAHAM, world-renowned Evangelist, in partaking of a good old Southern style country ham breakfast at the Biltmore Hotel this morning. . . The breakfast was given by a group of 212 TENNESSEANS who had come by special train from NASHVILLE, to attend the GRAHAM Crusade in Memorial Coliseum here. . . The TENNESSEANS brought along center slices of the choicest country ham from the VOLUNTEER state, grits, sorghum molasses and biscuits (they had them baked in Nashville and flown to Los Angeles by jet for the breakfast). Red-eye gravy was a menu feature. There were 350 persons present. Billy Graham was the first speaker. He was followed by Roy Rogers and his lovely wife Dale. "Pek" Gunn, leader of the Tennessee group, served as Master of Ceremonies. Presentations of two genuine Tennessee country hams were made. One went to Billy Graham, with HOWARD HOOPER, Co-Chairman of the Tennessee delegation, presenting. Mrs. Richard M. "Pek" Gunn, Secretary to the Special Train Committee, presented the other ham to Dale and Roy. . . A giant-sized check, the shape of Tennessee, 2½ feet wide by 6 feet long, in the amount of $2500.00 made out to the BILLY GRAHAM EVANGELISTIC ASSOCIATION, was presented by Gunn, the Rev. James M. Gregg, Co-Chairman of the Tennessee group, and Hooper. Gunn used the following verse in the presentation of the check. Mr. Graham accepted for the Association.

When we think of all your kindness
    Shown to us throughout the years;
How you shared with us our gladness,
    Stood by us in all our tears.

We are debtors and we feel it;
    We can never hope to pay
For the kindness heaped upon us
    By you folks from day to day.

With this gift now we're not trying
    To repay the debt as such;
Won't you take it as a token
    That we love you very much......

ACKNOWLEDGMENT

TO

WILLIAM CARROL and BETTY EMILINE GUNN, deceased; my parents who taught me obedience to parental authority; and to the laws of GOD and Country. Who instilled into me principles that I treasure more highly today than all the material wealth that they might have left me had they been very, very wealthy. . . . Papa always said: "TELL THE TRUTH IF IT TAKES THE HIDE"; while Mama's motto was: "IN HIS PURE EYES IT IS A SIN TO STEAL A PENNY OR A PIN"; and she always said: "A PERSON IS KNOWN BY THE COMPANY HE KEEPS."

TO

My older sisters, Bertie and Irene, earnest, sincere Christian persons who thought "PEK" was the greatest brother in all the world.

TO

My baby sister WILLIE MAE, who still lives at the old home place with her family. "BILL," as I always called her, is the most unselfish person I have ever known.

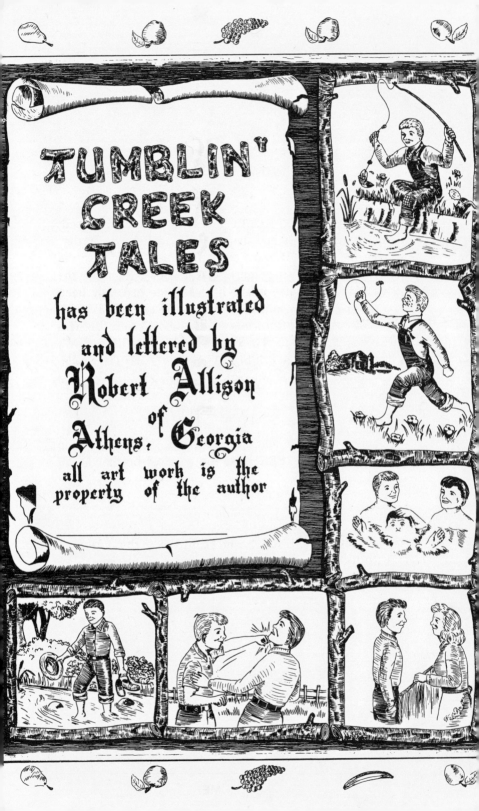

MARCH 12, 1970

"Pek" Gunn, poet laureate of the State of Tennessee, is a man whose soul, like a mountain stream, bubbles through life, cleansing and refreshing all it touches.

This is the man the founders of the United States envisioned as their descendant. This is the man for whom the pioneers overcame every privation in their great push from Atlantic to Pacific, for he is of their spirit.

Hear this man—in his formal addresses, in his after-dinner talks, in his poetry, his prose, and his music.

Hear this man and you will never despair over the future of mankind.

Hear this man and you will be a stronger and happier person the next day.

Bill Surber
A copy-Editor For
The St. Louis Post-Dispatch

An American's American

I had a long chat with Richard M. Gunn, widely known as "Pek," over several cups of coffee and the poet laureate of Tennessee was in rare form. This author, humorist, columnist and speaker is in the process of having a new book of poems published and if you have missed his "Tales From Tumbling Creek," you should correct this oversight immediately. "Pek" Gunn is a living example of the American story, the American dream. As he describes it, "My homeplace could best be described as three rooms and a path to the plumbing." His boyhood was one of adversity and poverty. His first paying job was "40¢ a day and keep," and keep was corn pone, turnip greens, and sow belly. To quote the articulate Mr. Gunn, "I didn't realize it at the time, but each seemingly insurmountable obstacle served as a stepping stone to success as it was conquered." It was this dogged determination, refusing to accept defeat, with eyes on a far brighter horizon, that made men like our poet laureate and in the process made America. To those of our impoverished population, I would recommend that you cease crying on someone's shoulder about your lack of opportunity and use your own shoulder to carry your share of the load—using each stumbling block on your path to the top as a stepping stone. Anyone can drift with the current, but to move upstream you've got to use your oar.

W. Paul Redick
Director Special Schools
Americana Series WENO Radio